TEACH YOUR CHILD TO SPELL

John S. Cheetham is Director of the Student
Achievement Centre, a private educational
and psychological consulting group in Melbourne, Australia. John is an experienced
primary and secondary teacher. As a counsel-
lor and teacher, John has worked with
numerous people in creating a solution to
spelling difficulties.

The Student Achievement Centre assesses
and works with students from a variety of
schools who encounter difficulties with their
learning. The Centre also conducts residential
workshops for parents and students on
effective learning, study and examination
techniques.

If you'd like to share your experiences
in using this method, write to: John
Cheetham, Director, Student Achievement
Centre, Box 478, Cheltenham, 3192,
Australia.

Teach
Your Child
to Spell

JOHN S. CHEETHAM
B.A., B.Ed., F.S.S.E., M.A.C.E.

HYLAND HOUSE

First published in 1990 by
Hyland House Publishing Pty Limited
10 Hyland Street
South Yarra
Victoria 3141
Reprinted 1991

National Library of Australia
Cataloguing-in-publication data:

Cheetham, J. S.
  Teach your child to spell.

  ISBN 0 947062 40 8.

  1. English language—Orthography and spelling—Study and teaching (Primary). I. Title.

372.63

Illustrations by Miranda Welch
The photographs in this book are by Don Whyte
All the children in the photographs are models.
The teacher is Mrs Carol Robbins.
Typeset by Solo Typesetting, South Australia
Printed by Australian Print Group, Maryborough, Victoria

FOREWORD

A child's parents are its natural teachers or, as today's language has it, primary caregivers. Under their guidance the child learns many of the fundamental lessons of life at the appropriate developmental stages.

How sad it is, then, that when the youngster encounters difficulties in formal language tasks, particularly spelling, so often the adult feels helpless and unsure, believing that only the school or highly skilled outside professional help can solve the problem.

Certainly there are situations in which such assistance should and must be sought but frequently, particularly at early primary level, help at home can be most effective. Generally it is the child's caregivers who have the insight into its character, temperament and needs that successful sustained improvement requires. All that is missing is some guidance for the helpers.

This useful little book sets out clearly a simple but dynamic method of building up skill and confidence in spelling. It offers a framework for turning losers into winners and at the same time strengthening family bonds. With its support much can be done to enable children to overcome spelling problems before they create other major language troubles. In this way a normal happy educational growth can be fostered.

ANGELA M. RIDSDALE, PH.D.
Monash University
March 1990

CONTENTS

ACKNOWLEDGEMENTS

The author would like to thank the following persons:

Mr George Rayner, the Melbourne Ear, Nose and Throat Specialist who provided insights into the auditory process and who threw down the gauntlet for something to be done for chronic poor spellers.

Mrs Carol Robbins who has taught, evaluated and helped me to develop this system with 400 students and their parents over the last eight years.

Dr Angela Ridsdale of Monash University, who made many supportive and helpful suggestions, based on her experience as a teacher at primary, secondary and tertiary levels.

Mr Patrick Smyth, who tested the ideas and shaped the manuscript, both with students and at the editor's desk.

Dr Barry Mollenhauer, who was constantly generous with his technical advice and computer expertise.

My wife Bobbie, and daughters Sarah and Natalie, who allowed me to 'hide' on family holidays so that I could have time to write.

Anne Greig, our secretary, who is ever patient and puts things into perspective with her humour.

INTRODUCTION

Spelling and the acquisition of the rules of spelling can cause great difficulty for students. Why?

There are many exceptions to spelling rules in English, partly due to the input of many foreign language words and sounds. An example of the difference in sound from the one combination are the **ea** words, e.g. beat, dread, great. This can cause problems in spelling.

However, parents tell us that the most common difficulties they experience in helping their children to learn spelling are:

- the child's reluctance, which forces the parents into nagging and insisting that the spelling work be done so it becomes almost a punishment, and
- poor memory for the words learnt from day to day.

It is a common belief that spelling comes naturally: 'You either have a gift for learning words or you don't'. This is not our view.

Most of the students with whom we have worked see spelling as a chore imposed on them by the school so their spelling work is rushed through in the hope, no doubt, that 'out of sight is out of mind' — and that's exactly what happens! Many students forget how to spell a word as quickly as they learn it or, even worse, they only partly learn the word in the first place.

There are many reasons why people have difficulty with spelling. This book does not aim to solve all spelling difficulties. It does, however, provide a workable method for parents to try to help their children to overcome their resistance to learning spelling and so to improve their spelling performance.

As well as improving spelling you will receive the bonus of a new relationship with your child in its learning. Parents who have used the technique described in this book, have often told us how their child has:

- become more open in talking about what is happening at school,
- become more communicative with both parents,
- developed a willingness to try learning activities — and even become enthusiastic about homework — which previously had been thought of as 'too difficult' and so often avoided,
- developed competency with spelling leading to more enthusiasm for writing.

IS THIS THE BOOK FOR ME?

In order to get the best from the technique this book teaches, you will need to find out whether your child has the following four skills before you begin teaching the new method. Check to see that your child can:

(1) Recognise all the letters of the alphabet by name and sound.

(2) Write the alphabet from memory in the correct order, in both capital and small letters.

(3) Be able to tell the difference between a long and short vowel sound, e.g., cap—cape; bon—bone. Show them the following pairs of words. Can they read them correctly?

a	e	i	o	u
tap	pet	bit	not	cut
tape	Pete	bite	note	cute

(4) Identify and correctly pronounce the pairs of letters which together represent a sound in speech, e.g. **ow** as in the *digraph* thr**ow**, or **oa** as in the *diphthong* b**oa**t. For a full list see page 64.

We find at the Student Achievement Centre that really poor spellers do much better in this method after they have mastered these four skills. Some suggestions for helping them master these skills will be found in Appendix B.

ALL ABOUT SPELLING

There are twenty-six letters in the English language. Five of these are vowels (**a e i o u**) and the remaining letters are consonants; **y** is sometimes used as a vowel, replacing **i** or **e**. These twenty-six letters combine to make forty-five sounds in spoken English. For further explanation of how words are built in the English language, see pages 60–4.

To be able to spell a word you need to be able to **say it correctly**. Words are built up (*encoded*) or broken down (*decoded*) into their *sound* parts. For example, the *decoded* phrase **mod-el tr-ai-n** can be *encoded* as **model train**.

Phonics is a method of teaching reading, pronunciation and spelling by associating letters and combinations of letters with their appropriate speech sounds, using encoding and decoding skills.

Decoding skills help children to attack words and break them down into parts.

The seven stages of such decoding skills are the ability to recognise:

(1) Initial vowel sounds: **a**pple **e**gg **i**nk.
(2) Initial consonant sounds: **b**oat **h**at **j**ump.
(3) Short middle vowel sounds: p**e**t h**o**p s**i**t.
(4) Long vowel sounds: t**a**pe n**o**te b**i**te.
(5) Initial consonant blends and digraphs: **sh**ed **sl**ip **sp**ot.
(6) Final consonant blends and digraphs: se**nd** ha**ng** wi**th**.
(7) Vowel digraphs and diphthongs: r**oo**m h**ea**rd t**ai**l.

Spelling is built up through being able to 'hear and see' particular combinations of sounds. The sound unit is the key to decoding written words. In English, **a sound** can be spelt with one letter, or two, three or four letters in combination, e.g.

1 letter **c**	**c**-a-t
2 letters **cl**	**cl**-i-ck
3 letters **oar**	b-**oar**-d
4 letters **ough**	b-**ough**

You can assist your child's development of this skill by using flashcards containing nonsense combinations and the sound groups so that the child *enjoys* sight recognition. This helps to develop an internal set of rules which the child can use to master future blending and decoding activities (see Appendix B).

If your child has difficulty doing the tasks described at the start of this section, then some activities which you can use are suggested in Appendix B. The child should have mastered these skills before going on to learn the spelling technique that this book teaches.

SOME REASONS FOR PROBLEMS WITH SPELLING

Difficulties with spelling can arise for the child who has:

(1) problems with long term memory,
(2) a visual difficulty which means that the picture of the word in the child's mind is not clear enough to be remembered and reproduced correctly,
(3) a developmental delay (specific learning disability of some form),
(4) failed to learn satisfactorily the sounds of spelling at school,
(5) a permanent or even intermittent hearing loss,
(6) neurological damage at birth or through an accident.

We have found that some 'mild' forms of hearing loss or visual loss, often described by a doctor or optometrist as 'insignificant', can affect a child's rate of progress in developing reading or spelling skills, mainly because the child fails to hear or see as well as the other children so their mistakes cause them to lose confidence and they learn to fail.

Children with permanent hearing loss and neurological damage may not respond to the technique described in this book. If you are in doubt about your child's ability to learn, or fear that there is some 'undiagnosed' block to learning, seek a professional assessment from a qualified educational psychologist or special education consultant.

WHY DO WE TEACH THIS WAY?

THE 'MISSED BOAT' SYNDROME
In 1980, a leading Australian Ear, Nose and Throat Specialist, Mr George Rayner alerted me to the problems caused by the 'missed boat' syndrome, a condition which he believed resulted from frequent early childhood ear infections, often accompanied by tonsil and adenoid problems.

EDUCATIONAL EFFECTS
Some hearing loss between three and six years of age may result from ear infection and this minimal amount of early childhood deafness is often easy to miss or ignore. Mr Rayner's view is that a hearing loss of 15 to 20 decibels for six months during this age span will be sufficient to produce a disruption to the formation of words and their spelling. This in turn creates a long term handicap in learning the difference between sounds and the ability to blend sounds together to form words.

This handicap occurs because children miss the vital experience of putting 'sound and picture' together in their effort to master words. Children so affected have a low response rate to both the conventional and the usual remedial methods of teaching spelling; they seem, throughout their school days, to remain very weak spellers. It is thought that this could be the result of an interference to the formation of the word centre in their brain, due to the temporary hearing loss that has occurred.

EFFECTS ON THE FAMILY

This temporary hearing loss can occur without the parent or child being particularly aware of it and can occur for only one child in a family, where all the other children are managed in the same way. Sometimes parents feel guilty when they discover what has happened and it is important to avoid falling into the trap of feeling unnecessarily guilty if you want to help your child.

EFFECTS ON THE CHILD

For the child who has experienced a temporary hearing loss, the missing information or knowledge about language is something that has been lost and cannot easily be replaced. Even though the child's hearing returns to normal levels, the problem caused by the temporary loss remains.

REMEDYING THE PROBLEM

It is like building a house which must have a foundation. A house without proper foundation is in risk of collapsing. This particular child's language is similar. We must lay firm foundations (correct the long term handicap). If we concentrate on the walls and roof (reading) there won't be much long term benefit if the foundation is still unstable or inappropriate!

Many parents whose children have had remedial help can't understand why their child's language keeps collapsing. Often, as we explain to them, it is because there was little solid foundation. The technique you are now learning will help to build the foundation for your child which may have been missing or poorly constructed.

WHAT THE STUDENT ACHIEVEMENT CENTRE DOES

For the last eight years we have experimented with strategies to assist children with spelling problems and this technique for teaching spelling results largely from that work. It has been successfully used with students from six to sixteen years old. The only cases known to us to have failed, in the long term, have been those where the technique was:

- rushed, and short cuts attempted, or
- unable to be grasped by parents who couldn't form a positive and patient working relationhip with their child, or
- replaced by old habits of learning spelling, or
- abandoned in the belief that the poor speller was 'cured' and could return prematurely to learning spelling in more conventional ways.

It is our view that one reason this technique is highly successful is because it provides an ingredient which is missing from most remedial techniques: **it is done daily.**

'SPELLING IS DUMB AND I'M HOPELESS AT IT'

Children with a spelling problem see classroom failure as a poor reward for any effort put in at home, and become despondent when asked to learn more words the next day. After a short time they are saying, 'Spelling is dumb and I am hopeless at it,' and sinking into a role in life as a poor speller, believing that the gift of the gods has not been offered to them. In the long term this affects their written expression and they will avoid using words that could have been mastered if taught effectively. Soon the cry goes up that their written expression is immature, and before long they become increasingly reluctant to write stories or to engage in written expression activities with any conviction. Disenchantment with the written language leads to an unwillingness to try. In addition children often develop sloppy handwriting to conceal poor spelling.

With a number of children we have seen at the Centre, reluctance to read occurs when spelling difficulties have become long term. Why read when somebody is going to ask you to write something about what you have read? A barrier to participating and growing in language has been firmly placed across the child's educational path. After three or four years of this with poor results being obtained in written expression, spelling and reading, a decision to drop out of the more academic subjects is often made.

> We have yet to meet a child who **chooses** to be a poor speller. Show them that good spelling is possible and watch the motivation return.

Although a non-academic system of education may well be to these children's advantage, poor language skill development leads to long term problems, no matter what the vocational choice. A number of trades people and businessmen have come to us, as adults, over the years, and asked for help with their poor reading and spelling. It is obvious that an ability to communicate effectively is an advantage to everybody, no matter what career they choose to follow. Not only is this true in the vocational area, but it is also true in the area of inter-personal relationships. The ability to feel comfortable with language as a means of expressing what you think and feel will enhance communication with family and friends. An inability to do so creates tension for the individual and those around them, and often leads to more desperate measures being used to get somebody else to understand their feelings.

HOW OUR TECHNIQUE FITS INTO NORMAL CLASSROOM LEARNING

Our technique works well with other means of developing word knowledge. It is important to stress that it is designed as a remedial technique to help children who can't spell because of the 'missed boat' syndrome. However, it has proved successful with poor spellers in general. It is not suggested that the technique also become a general classroom teaching technique, or even replace conventional sequential spelling programs. **Its usefulness is exclusively for working in a 1:1 situation with a chronic poor speller.**

If your child is a poor reader and part of the reading difficulty is caused by a lack of decoding skills, then this book may be used in conjunction with a school program to develop decoding skills. An understanding of these skills—how language is built—is essential, in our view, to the development and acquisition of reading and spelling skills.

LOOK OUT FOR THESE PROBLEMS

If you force children continually to stumble through unsuitable reading material every night you will simply give them further messages of frustation, fatigue and disappointment. No wonder such children go back to school next day even more depressed about the impossibility of learning and it is not surprising that they are often reported by teachers as being 'lacking in motivation', 'untidy workers', 'distractable and distracting' or as having 'poor concentration'. Under these circumstances, the relationship between parent and child can deteriorate.

If children have reading skills two years or more behind their class level, or have evident difficulty with decoding skills or spelling, we recommend that you don't try to get them to read until the decoding skills are consolidated and this spelling program has been under way for 2 to 3 months.

Parents are often told that the more their children read the better they will become. This may be true for children who have not suffered from the 'missed boat' syndrome, or from severe visual difficulties that have interfered with their language learning. But most children with spelling difficulties gain little more than frustration and loss of confidence in themselves as learners if too much stress is placed on reading activity too early in the program.

If the school is sending home material for your child to read which is too difficult for the child's present stage of achievement and does not draw upon the decoding skills you are currently teaching in your spelling program, why not try reading the material aloud to the child?

Don't keep the school in the dark. Let your child's teachers know what you are doing and ask for their co-operation in cutting down on material being sent home during those early days. After all, it's only for a short time.

The child's interest in books and what they offer can be kept up by:
- reading to the child,
- having them listen to taped stories,
- reading 'How To' books, and
- providing magazines, such as car and rock publications that will interest the child.

SOME POINTS TO KEEP IN MIND

The parent teaching spelling by this method should never forget that:
- If children are failing they are not likely to keep on working in that situation.
- Children who are used to failure need instant success in a new activity or they will give up easily.
- Failure causes a negative attitude and anxiety, which makes the brain speed up. This 'speed up' will lead to confusion as the student's brain cannot clearly photograph and store the material. For example, if the brain is rushed through a great number of new words it won't be able to unscramble the images it has been given so that the loss of words and jumbling of letters will occur more frequently.
- Learning spelling by looking at a word and then saying it aloud will often cause poor visual retention

because the sound interferes with the image in the mind.

- Learning spelling by writing the same word over and over again is boring and results in poor performance. You don't have to think to endlessly copy out words automatically. It just puts the child off the process of learning spelling.

- Children who are bored will 'switch off'. When the brain is switched off it doesn't learn and the children are not consciously focusing on the structure of the word. They become dulled to the way in which words are constructed and tend to miss commonly recurring patterns of letters.

- Some people believe that children will grow out of difficulties with spelling, but this rarely happens. Generally children become worse, not better, since they soon accept the fact that they are a failure and so cease to try. Help is needed to reverse the position.

- Practice every day is essential to good learning. If this technique is used daily it establishes new habits and fosters memory. This means that the helping adult is absolutely necessary to the success of the method.

- Children learn better and become more confident and enthusiastic if they don't feel stressed or threatened. Our technique will teach you how to develop a positive attitude for your student in reading and spelling activities.

WHY THE TECHNIQUE WORKS

The technique is based on an approach where more than one channel into the brain is used to assist learning. These channels are vision, hearing and touch.

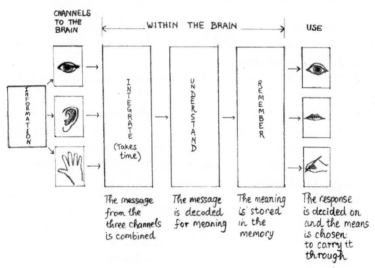

CHANNELS TO THE BRAIN

1. The adult who is working with the child takes control of what the child is doing by adopting a special teaching position and systematically exposing parts of the word for the child to focus on (see page 35).

The children are not left to learn spelling on their own, nor are they sent away to learn words and return to have them checked. They learn under the direct supervision of the person working with them. This ensures that the adult knows what is happening to a word or part of a word at any given time. It also means that the adult's personality and attitude can be used to relieve anxiety on the part of the learner and control the pace of learning. This seems to work particularly well if the adult has constant contact with the child who is then happy to please and will want to enjoy a positive relationship with the helper.

The key to this system is: **the slower the child learns, the more effectively the brain will store what is being learnt.**

2. Because you have written the word in parts in large, well spaced writing, the children only see the part exposed at any one time.

Each part is exposed for two to three seconds, so that the children gain a clear picture of that part, and can store it before the next part is introduced. Because of this controlled **slowing down** of the information presented children absorb the word in a systematic way. Our observations have revealed that many poor spellers use eye movements similar to the following:

	elephant
1st look	el - eph - an - t
2nd look	el - ep - hant
3rd look	e - lep - hant

Notice what the child has done on looking at the word elephant. The first look at the word, which is usually learnt as a whole word, yields el-eph-an-t. The second look yields el-ep-hant. The third look yields e-lep-hant.

What will the brain remember?

The child has fed in three different photographs of the same thing, none of which is consistent with any of the others.

To make matters worse children usually rush across the word, and each photograph takes 1.5 to 2 seconds for the whole word—barely enough time to draw breath, let alone effectively remember what was being taken in. In addition, when you ask them to spell a word, most of the concentration probably goes into saying the letters out loud by name, e.g. e-l-e-p-h-a-n-t, rather than in blending the sounds of the word together. As a result the children, when attempting to spell a word from memory, will often end up with all the letters mixed up. With luck the word may be successfully spelled in the short term, but ask again tomorrow morning and the brain may well have completely lost the image of the word because it was poorly fed into the brain in the first place. Hence the cry, 'He knew how to spell it last night but he failed his spelling test at school today.'

The brain is divided into two halves. These are called the *left hemisphere* and the *right hemisphere*. The hemispheres are joined by the *corpus callosum*. Information from each hemisphere passes back and forth through the corpus callosum. Each hemisphere is responsible for processing information differently. Look at the 'bird's eye view' below:

THE BRAIN

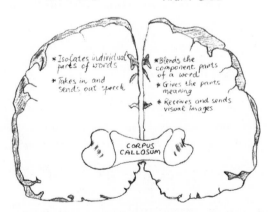

LEFT SIDE   RIGHT SIDE

* Isolates individual parts of words
* Takes in and sends out speech

* Blends the component parts of a word
* Gives the parts meaning
* Receives and sends visual images

CORPUS CALLOSUM

THE TWO HALVES OF THE BRAIN PLAY IMPORTANT ROLES IN SPELLING

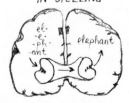

el-
-e-
-ph-
-ant   elephant

Children who have a temporary hearing loss may, like deaf children, suffer an interrupted flow of information between the left and right hemispheres of the brain. There are other parts of the brain that help in language formation and its use. However, for our purposes, this simplified description of how the right and left hemispheres cooperate to enable children to learn and remember spelling may provide helpful background to understanding what our technique of teaching spelling is designed to do.

SOME HABITS TO BREAK

- Stop children learning spelling on their own. Let them learn with your supervision.
- Stop children looking at words and saying them aloud, then repeating the word letter by letter; this practice makes it difficult for them to hold a mental picture of the word.
- Ignore any errors that children may make. This reduces the stress in attempting to learn words. Errors are fine. We don't care if they occur, so we *never* comment on them. Such comments as:

'Hurry up',

'You've seen that word before',

'Watch what you're doing',

'Concentrate, you got it right a minute ago',

'Why don't you look at what you're doing?'

will create a negative attitude and children will panic in an attempt to please you. Panic leads to a faster work pace, but our technique emphasises that the slower children work, the more likely they are to succeed and recall the word in the long term.

WORK SLOWLY

Encourage the child to develop the habit of working as slowly as possible.

Don't teach more than 5 to 6 words per night. Attempting to learn 20 words in one sitting will lead to confusion and poor recall.

If your school issues 20 words a week then that is a considerable advantage. If it expects 20 words to be learnt per night then talk with your child's classroom teacher and negotiate a slower pace in the interest of your child *not* developing a problem and reluctance with spelling. By learning 5 to 6 words a night your child's brain will have a chance to store them before you pump in additional words. Stress for the child is also reduced if there are only a few words to be done in the one sitting. Result? You will notice that your child becomes less anxious and more motivated to improve spelling. There is also less stress for the adult involved and there is more chance of a genuinely beneficial working relationship being fostered.

USE SMALL UNITS
Why do children with poor short term memories respond well to this technique?

Take our new word, 'elephant'. It has eight letters in sequence. Children with poor short term visual memories can usually recall three, four or even five letters in sequence, but after that they begin to become confused. So what is likely to happen when you introduce eight letters in sequence? You guessed it! Confusion and stress. Once children become confused or stressed they become angry and resentful, and tend to rush what they are doing.

We want them to work slowly. You will find out on the pages that follow, that the most the child will have to recall is 3 to 4 units of information at any one time, e.g. 'elephant' will be broken down into **el-e-ph-ant**, and only one part exposed at any one time. Hence the maximum number of letters to remember is 3 units—**ant**—and this should be manageable for most children. The way in which words are broken down into groups of units will be explained later.

PRE-TESTING
Finally, before commencing the spelling session **each night**, give the child an incentive. This will be different from the benefit which you see as an adult. Your goal is increased literacy for your child. Getting out to play fifteen minutes earlier might be a much more attractive reward for a child!

- Save time by pre-testing (page 38).
- Invite your child to let you test the words which are to be learnt.
- Give the child a pen and paper and say, 'Let's check to see if you know any of these words already. That will save you time, as there is no point in learning what you already know and you might like to do other things.'

This is a marvellous boost for children's confidence since usually there will be one word that they may know or at least get partially right.

A HABIT TO BREAK

> Never hear a child spell a word out loud.

A HABIT TO START

> Sell the benefit of what you're doing to the child.

THE DAILY DRILL

An advantage of this method for the child is that you work on it for ten to fifteen minutes per day, six days per week. That is equivalent to about one to two hours of solid work with spelling each week. Each period is short enough for the child not to lose interest nor to become bored. As you are controlling what is happening, even children with a concentration problem can usually work under supervision for this amount of time.

Resentment is minimised because no comment is made if mistakes occur, so there is no pressure on the child beyond the ability to sit for ten to twenty minutes with you, six days a week.

Daily repetition, with a break of one day a week, is essential to progress. To develop a skill, practise it daily. Sportspersons learnt this a long time ago.

> Remember, ten minutes per day is much more effective than one single session per week.

It is a myth that this daily drill creates pressure for children if they have been working at school during the day. What really creates pressure for the child is using a system which is inefficient, and leads to frustration and poor results, which in turn elicit negative comments from teachers and parents.

This situation must be reversed and then learning becomes possible. The most potentially powerful influence on the child to start this change is the parent. As pressure on the child increases, the child will look to the parent for emotional support to relieve the negative feelings which build up through school failure. If parents can convert their own concern, disappointment and frustration into positive encouragement for the child, then the child is better able to learn.

Nothing succeeds like success, and when the child sees spelling test results that reflect a greater competency, the desire to continue with the daily habit will be fostered.

Be alert to the results of tests given at school. Any improvement, even just a single mark, should be noted and the child's attention drawn to it. Explain that the improvement proves that change is possible. Many children become despondent because of careless teacher and parental comments like: 'You got six out of ten, imagine what you could do if you tried' or, 'That's OK, but you can do better on your next test.'

INVEST IN ENCOURAGEMENT

> The comments you make to a child can be either like a magic wand or a cudgel.

You are investing time in your child's improvement. Today, spelling may be difficult for your child, tomorrow it may be some crisis in adult life that needs to be faced and overcome, so time spent building up confidence in tackling the spelling obstacle will also be a training for developing confidence in facing other obstacles. If children have learnt to conquer one difficulty, they will be prepared to tackle other difficulties in later life. Why? Because they have learnt that they can win if they find the appropriate technique.

Working with a parent can be a vital key to energising children who lack the will to win.

Children who are failing in a key aspect of their schooling will absorb anxiety, thus blocking their learning of that task. As the negative feelings about a learning task increase, the ability of the brain to think clearly decreases. The relationship can be seen as:

EMOTIONS (Feeling)   INTELLECT (Thinking)

Negative feelings = Decreased ability to learn

and remember words

A parent can increase children's positive feelings by noticing and commenting on any *small* and worthwhile thing that they do. Everything that brings a smile or positive comment from the parent nurtures their good feelings about themselves. Never underestimate your power to help swing children away from feeling inadequate about their ability to tackle difficult tasks. Your aim as a parent is to increase the number of positive feelings that the child has *instead of* expecting too much progress with the child's learning.

The change that a parent is seeking to create is:

EMOTIONS (Feeling)   INTELLECT (Thinking)

Positive feelings = Increased ability
                         to learn
                    and remember words

Once a breakthrough has been made and children want to learn, and feel confident that they can, then a suitable technique will be needed for exposing the child to new knowledge. If the parent can acquire this technique then a positive change in spelling will occur.

CURRENT SITUATION

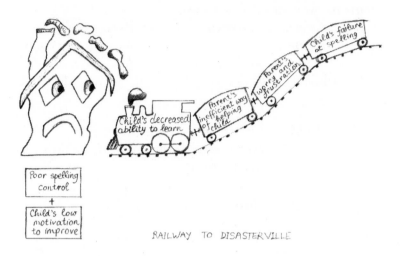

RAILWAY TO DISASTERVILLE

NEW SITUATION

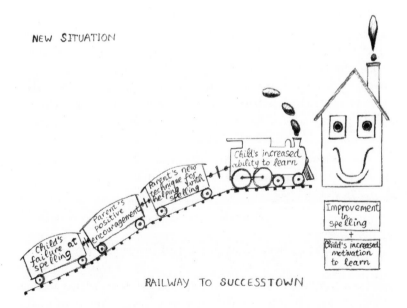

RAILWAY TO SUCCESSTOWN

WHO SHOULD TEACH THE CHILD?
1. Choose the parent who is regularly available and who wants to carry out the technique.

This program requires a commitment from the parent to be available for at least 15 minutes a day to work with the child. Your commitment is a positive investment in your child's growth and development. Your child needs you.

There is no reason why the task can't be shared by both parents. Problems occur only when the relieving parent is not completely familiar with the technique. This can cause a disruption in learning.

> Old habits come back quickly.
> New habits are slow to develop.

An unprepared parent can re-start old habits within ten minutes, and the regular teaching parent will find it difficult to train the child out of them. Also children become very frustrated with a relieving parent who is not competent with the technique. These difficulties can be avoided by having both parents working with the child for two nights before the relieving parent continues alone.

> For primary school students this technique should be used for a maximum of 15 minutes per day, six days per week.

2. The liaison between school and home is important.

Make an effort to work in conjunction with and with the cooperation of the class teacher. If your child's class teacher administers spelling tests, ask whether your child can be given some short term, special consideration, especially if the tests are conducted at a fast pace.

Our method encourages the child to work **slowly** and effectively to gain the necessary training in cueing correct responses. It often takes children *quite a few seconds* to close their eyes and cue themselves into the word. A quickly administered class test will not provide that opportunity and rushed, haphazard and incorrect responses are the most likely outcome. Then old habits will re-emerge and the child will become despondent if no improvement is seen in the classroom.

> Genuine inability to learn is rare. Most children can learn. It all depends on how they are taught.

THE TECHNIQUE— STEP-BY-STEP

At first this method may look complicated. It is not. Read it over patiently and you will see that it is straightforward. At the Student Achievement Centre it takes us about two hours to teach a parent to use it. Sometimes it helps to familiarise yourself with the technique if you read through a section a few times and then practise with someone checking it for you before you begin with your pupil. Once you've mastered the technique you will find that it will flow smoothly.

1. THE ENVIRONMENT AND THE TEACHING POSITION

Before you start make sure that your pupil is not hungry or thirsty and doesn't want to go to the toilet.

Select a quiet room without other family members, television or other distractions. **Privacy and quietness are essential to success.**

The teaching position is designed so that the parent or teacher has maximum control over the learning situation. Mistakes can be corrected quickly and the student's approach can be monitored easily. Any clues picked up by the person teaching can be acted upon without delay.

Opposite: The correct teaching position.

Loss of concentration is indicated by the child's gaze wandering about the room. If this happens tap the next part of the word with your finger to re-focus the student's gaze. Constantly wandering eyes and restless body movements may mean that you are trying to achieve too much in one session and that the child is becoming overloaded. Resume later or the next day. Cut down on the number of words per session. **Slow down.**

Sitting opposite the child enables you to monitor eye movements.

2. SELECTING THE WORDS

Depending on the age of your child and year level at school we suggest the following means of word selection:

(1) a spelling list set by the class teacher, or, if there is none, it might be a good idea to consult the teacher for help in making one up,
(2) regularly review the child's work books and make up a list of words commonly misspelt, and/or
(3) select words from the child's school readers or library books.

3. PRE-TESTING THE WORDS

Explain to the child the benefit of pre-testing, e.g. 'If we test the words before we begin, that will save you time. You won't have to learn words that you already know.'

Then ask the child to write the words on paper. Choose the words that are misspelt for the preparation described below. Praise the child for the words correctly spelt. If all the words are misspelt, congratulate the child on the effort made. Don't leave children wondering if they've done well or badly.

4. PREPARING THE WORDS

On a blank white page write the word in full, and underneath it break the word into segments. To begin with, the adult can break the word up but as children's confidence grows they may like to help break up a word. This active involvement by the child is a real step towards mastery of spelling.

elephant
el e ph ant

Opposite: Writing the word.

elephant

el e ph ant

5. BREAKING UP THE WORDS

    (1) Look for the common parts and the easy-to-see and remember bits.

ac	com	mo	date
Pt1	Pt2	Pt3	Pt4

    (2) Work from both ends of the word.

    (3) Always separate double consonants.

This word has been broken into 4 parts. By working from the right hand side the common word 'date' can be recognised and separated. All the double consonants **cc/mm** have been separated.

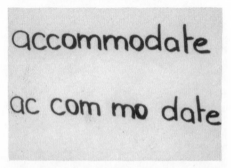

The word **accommodate** ready for teaching.

    (4) When treating words beginning with silent letters, such as 'wrong', 'knife', and 'wrapped', separate the silent letter from the other letters (see next page).

w rap ped

k ni fe

k ni ght

    (5) Space the word parts across the page.

    (6) Use a blank sheet of paper in preference to ruled paper. Use a red or yellow felt pen and write the full word in lettering of approximately 40 mm (1¾″) in height. Underneath the full word, using the same felt pen, write the parts of the word in a well spaced fashion. Remember to leave room to

cover up the full word and the different parts of the word, see below.

A4 Blank Paper

> elephant
>
> el e ph ant

red/yellow lettering

(7) As children become familiar with this technique, you may find that they will help you to break up the words.

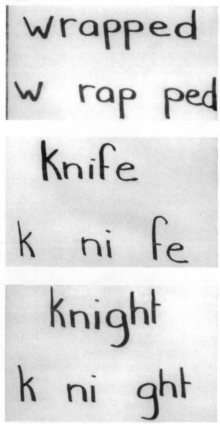

Words that start wit
silent letters.

6. THE TEACHING METHOD

(1) Sit opposite the child.

In this way you can comfortably expose the word and its parts and also watch the way in which the child is responding.

Spend a couple of minutes making the child comfortable. If the child is tense or anxious be reassuring. Make certain you smile a lot. You are enjoying being with the child and the child will enjoy playing with these words.

Emphasise that the child is not going to be asked to do anything which is difficult.

Sit opposite the child when teaching.

(2) **To be able to spell a word you need to be able to say it correctly!**

Cover the broken-up word in full so that only the complete word is visible. If the child can't say the word in full do not delay; say it yourself and ask the child to read it to you and perhaps even to repeat it.

Make sure you are still smiling. The child will respond to your facial expressions. If you lose your smile and warmth you will confirm the child's fear that this is a difficult and serious business.

Cover up the broken word in full.

(3) **Cover up the full word,** and with a separate piece of paper cover up all but the first part of the broken-up word.

Cover up the full word.

(4) **Get the child to look at Part 1 'el' and say it.** Count quietly to yourself 'One hundred, two hundred, three hundred', to allow the child to look at the part-word for approximately three seconds. During this time the child should focus on that part of the word. Watch carefully to ensure the child isn't gazing elsewhere.

If necessary, say 'Keep looking at this part of the word so that your mind can photograph it.'

If the child is unable to pronounce the letters or blend them together, tell the child what they are and ask the child to repeat them.

Have the child look at Part 1, **el**, and say it.

Listen to the child's pronunciation to make sure it is clear. It may be necessary for you to over-emphasise the sound and repeat it a couple of times as the child watches your lips.

Slow down!

(5) **With a third piece of paper cover Parts 1, 3 and 4, and expose Part 2.** Repeat the method described in (4) above when you expose each of the four parts in turn, working from left to right.

Working through the word.

Watch your child's eye movements. Are they focused on the exposed part of the word? If not, tap your finger next to the exposed word part to re-focus the child's gaze. Don't say anything to the child about lack of concentration.

Focusing the child's attention if the gaze wanders.

(6) Having worked through the word in this way, start again at the first part of the word and repeat the entire process.

Remember, **do it slowly**. Silently count 'one hundred, two hundred, three hundred' between each exposure.

(7) Place a large piece of blank paper over the exposed word and its parts. Give the child a pen and ask the child to write the word 'elephant' very slowly in the parts in which it has just been learnt, leaving a space between the parts.

Don't let the child write the word with all the letters connected, even though the child may be tempted to demonstrate mastery of the full word.

Don't take short cuts. We are training children to see the word in its component parts and to cue themselves by using these parts, but it can take a long time before this becomes a habit, and we want to develop a habit.

Children differ so much that it is impossible to specify a time when you can revert to them spelling a word in full. We must leave that to your judgement.

The child writes the word in the parts learnt.

(8) Whether the child has succeeded or not:
- make eye contact with the child,
- smile, and
- say, 'A good start' or something suitably encouraging.

Praise and practice are the keys.

HOW MANY WORDS SHOULD BE LEARNT PER SESSION?

Don't be too ambitious. It is better to master two new words a day than to overload your child.

As a guide, five words per session should be the maximum. Covering too many words during a session can lead to confusion.

There are many days ahead. Using this technique to teach 2 to 3 words a day means that your child will be able to spell 600 new words correctly in a year. Was that much achieved in the previous year?

7. OVERCOMING MEMORY BLOCKS

Don't delay in taking action if the child is stuck and has a memory block. You want to avoid frustration on the part of the learner so take the following steps:

(1) Take the pen from the child's hand.

Take the pen from the child's hand.

(2) Ask the child to close eyes.
(3) Relax and reassure the child. Tell children that it doesn't matter if they can't recall the information. It's a game. Make it fun. The more enjoyment you are getting the more motivated your student will be. Just be quietly confident in your mind that at some stage the child will grasp the spelling.

Relax the child.

(4) Take the hand that the child **writes with**. As you flatten the palm of that hand, say the word in full. Then tap out each part of the word on the palm of the hand, using one tap for each part, e.g. ac-com-mo-date would have four taps. **Make sure that the child's eyes are closed.**

Say to the child, 'Try to see the part of the word on the television set in your head as I tap it.'

Tap and say the word at the same time. Don't tap, then say. Saying the part should be timed to occur as your hand firmly taps the child's palm.

Count quietly to yourself 'one hundred, two hundred, three hundred' between each part to give the child an opportunity to practise it.

By asking the child to close the eyes we are removing the visual stimulus of looking around the room; by using the senses of touch (tapping) and hearing (saying the part of the word as we tap) we create a picture of the word in the mind. The child's concentration is upon re-creating this picture of the word in the mind.

(5) Repeat this once more so that you have gone over the word twice.

Tap and say the word parts simultaneously.

(6) Invite the child to rewrite the word twice **in the parts in which it was learnt**. Give the child the word in full so that the child can hear it completely, e.g. 'Please write the word "elephant" in its broken form.'

The child rewrites the word twice.

(7) If error recurs and the child experiences difficulty in picturing the word, start again.

Be reassuring and say to the child, 'That's fine. Let's just take it through again.'

Re-teach the word from the beginning of the teaching method on page 42.

Don't criticise or comment negatively on errors that the child makes.

There is a misguided view that if children are stuck they should be asked to make a number of attempts in the hope that they may stumble on the correct answer. For students who have not experienced long term learning difficulties this approach will not do any harm, but for students who have previously experienced difficulties then it is a quick way of discouraging them and increasing their stress.

Remember that it is an essential ingredient of working with children with a spelling problem that stress be reduced.

You will be able to recognise when your student is suffering stress from the following behaviour:

- wriggling,
- excessive moving in the chair,
- looking around the room,
- tapping hands or feet,
- frowning,
- blinking more rapidly,
- blushing,
- the tone of voice changing.

If you sit directly across the table from the student in the correct teaching position you will be able to observe these symptoms.

> If your child is stressed—STOP.

8. CONCLUDING EACH SESSION

At the end of the daily session try to give the child a feeling of hopefulness. A technique which many parents have found useful is to make a statement about how much they have enjoyed working with the child, rather than a statement about the child.

'That was fun, let's do it again, tomorrow!' will bring a warm response and build up the child's confidence.

Reinforce your statement with physical contact: a quick cuddle or hug, an arm around the shoulder or a pat on the back.

Reinforce your praise with physical contact.

Never underestimate the power of an encouraging spoken message, linked with warm physical contact. Even if the session has been a difficult one for the child, the memory that will last until the next session is one of warmth, enjoyment and genuine closeness with the parent.

It takes time to break down the stress and anxiety about learning spelling. However, stress and anxiety both affect the way in which the brain learns, hence we must get rid of them.

A child who has had little success with words in the past will not have much **inner motivation** to learn spelling.

External motivation can be a useful tool for the parent. Each activity that we do with the child has an immediate reward. As the child experiences more success with spelling tests at school the inner motivation will begin to take over. Thus we help to build the child's inner motivation by using our external power to reward the child. **Rewards should be discussed with the child.** They need to be something that has value or meaning for the child. The warm, physical contact mentioned above *may* be a reward in itself.

By using external motivation we focus the child's attention on a more realistic goal than being a **good speller**, which may take a long time to achieve. By concentrating on the task at hand the child gets an immediate benefit. Repeated performances help us to achieve our long-term goal.

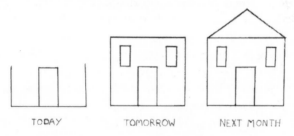

TODAY   TOMORROW   NEXT MONTH

FINAL GOAL :   A COMPETENT SPELLER

Each Day Is Building Your Child's Spelling

Immediate rewards are useful tools on our journey to good spelling.

9. NEXT DAY

(1) Start by testing the words taught the previous day. Explain the advantage to the child of doing this (see page 38).

Keep all the sheets of paper with the words on them in a box. As the child learns more words, select at random any handful for your pre-test so that all the words are reviewed at intervals. Try to revise all the words at least once every two weeks, even if this means using a couple of sessions for testing rather than teaching new words.

One of your aims should be to build up a base of newly acquired words that the child will begin to feel confident with and then start to use at school when writing stories or other written expression activities.

(2) This is the right time to discuss the meanings of the words. Don't teach meanings while teaching spelling. When the child is confident with the spelling you can introduce meanings. However, if the child asks the meaning of a word you should offer an explanation or definition of the word. Don't ignore a request for meaning.

(3) Introduce the new words for the day (3 to 4 words) as explained in 1–8 above.

> Reach the goal by methodically and slowly following these steps.

CONSOLIDATING THE ACHIEVEMENTS

After using this method for a couple of weeks, if you have time and your child is responsive, you might like to add some variety by trying these additional activities:

1. **Visually reinforcing the words helps the child to move from vision to sound.**
   - Put up a maximum of five newly learnt words on the back of the toilet door.

     Change the words every third day. Write the words on blank paper in large letters with the same felt-tipped pen that you have been using for the teaching sessions. The words may be written in full and, unless you so desire, they don't need to be broken into their teaching parts.

     Children on the toilet are a captive audience and it seems that the place where they most often focus their attention is on the back of the door. Words placed on bedroom walls, refrigerators and such places have to compete with other things so our recommendation is the toilet door.

2. **Linking reading with spelling helps the child to move from vision to sound.**
   - Take all the words your child has been learning with you and, using them together, make up a story or sentences incorporating the words. Invite the child to read the story or sentences with you.

3. **Dictation helps the child to move from sound to vision.**
   (1) Make up a short passage using the words learnt together. Occasionally the child may like to help

you make up a story orally, using the words learnt. You can then write the story down. It is recommended that the passage be no longer than five sentences.

(2) Ask the child to relax.

(3) Tell the child to close eyes.

(4) Invite the children to picture **the words** in their minds as you read the passage: 'As I read the story slowly, try to see each word as I say it.'

(5) Read the passage slowly.

(6) If children become anxious because it is 'difficult to see the words', reassure them that this is a skill which will develop.

If children are still anxious, invite them to read the passage to you. Don't let them stumble over the words; help if necessary.

(7) Slowly dictate to the child. If the child responds, correct the passage together. If not, encourage the child. Give the child a cuddle and conclude the session.

(8) Look at the passage after the child has left and note any errors that were made. Teach them correctly next day.

This is not a test. The reason for doing the dictation exercise is to consolidate the words and subtly to help the child to see the words in context. The child sees the words, not as isolated objects for a spelling lesson, but sees them 'at work', contributing to a meaning. This brings an added meaning to the learning process.

A STUDENT-FRIENDLY METHOD OF DICTATION

Suppose that the following words have been learnt:

music	week	straight
tribe	thirsty	just
wash	surprise	ground

Let us invent a short passage that makes sense using these words.

Every *week* I *wash* the car. The water runs *straight* onto the *ground*. Then I'm *thirsty* and I go down to the milk bar to buy a *surprise* and listen to the *music* with my *tribe*. It's *just* great!

The sentences could be presented as single sentences or as a story. Keep it simple. It doesn't have to be a literary masterpiece. Be careful not to include other words which will be too difficult for your student to write.

1. Read the passage slowly, as suggested above.
2. Sit opposite the child in the teaching position so you can observe as you dictate.

   (1) Read the first sentence slowly.
       'Every week I wash the car.'
   (2) Repeat part of the sentence slowly.
       'Every week . . .'
   (3) Then repeat the part read, adding the remainder of the sentence.
       'Every week I wash the car.'
   (4) Repeat the new part of the sentence slowly.
       'I wash the car.'
   (5) Then give the punctuation.
       'Full stop.'
   (6) The child can now write down the first sentence.
   (7) Dictate the other sentences in a similar fashion. Long sentences may be dictated in parts.
   (8) When you have finished, ask the child to relax, close eyes and listen to the passage as you re-read it. 'Close your eyes and try to see each word as I read it.'
   (9) Ask the child to open eyes and check the passage as you slowly read it once more.
       'Open your eyes, check it and make any alterations you want as I read.'
3. Finish with an encouraging comment and warm physical contact with the child. You could walk around

behind the child, give the child a pat on the shoulder or a hug and say, 'You've done very very well and tried very hard.'

MEASURING SUCCESS

As dictation at school is usually given as a test, you must be very sensitive to any anxiety created in the child. Work done as part of this technique, with a parent, should never resemble a test of how much has been learnt. Remember, even our pre-test of words done at the start of a session was explained as a benefit for the child, to *reduce* work, not to see how much has been learnt.

Formal assessments of progress in spelling are best left to the school. In this way the parent never has to change roles from 'helper' to 'judge'—such a change in the parental role would reawaken all the old anxieties that the child has about learning.

Also it is more satisfying for children when the school notes an improvement in work. It makes them feel good because they know that it is the school that is the judge of learning standards. It also enables them to come home to share with the parent the excitement of something jointly achieved.

For the parent, it is an act of faith! Ideally, your child has a sensitive and aware teacher so some praise will be forthcoming from the school.

Always avoid the temptation to measure your progress formally. You will already know, informally, what progress is being made by the child's response to the work that you are doing together. **You won't motivate by testing or judging. You'll destroy the child's faith in you as a helper.**

Measurement is not one of our teaching tools.

CONCLUSION

Once you have mastered this method you will be better able to help your child to spell. As we stated at the beginning of this book, the only time we have found that the technique doesn't work is when the more subtle aspects of the method have been missed or forgotten.

Review your teaching technique periodically by using the checklist in Appendix C and increase your chances of success.

Some parents, once they have become confident with our technique for teaching spelling, find it more convenient to use the abbreviated instructions in Appendix D. This is a quick memory stimulator that includes all stages of the technique. It is helpful also to use as a reference at the actual time of teaching.

As a parent, don't be discouraged if you need to go back and re-read this section.

Enjoy your time working with your child.

60

APPENDIX A— CHECKLIST FOR THE LEARNER

Can your child:

	YES	NO
• Write the alphabet from memory in correct sequence in capital letters small letters		

	YES	NO
• Recognise all the letters of the alphabet by name? sound?		

1.   If you find that the answer to any of these activities is 'No', you will need to begin by teaching the alphabet and the **names** and **sounds** of letters before going any further. See Appendix B for some suggestions for this. When the child can do these things, return to this section and read on.

2.   Having mastered the names and sounds of letters you can move on to develop your child's understanding of how sounds are made by combining different letters.

3.   In Appendix B you will find a list of nonsense combinations of letters that will help the child to learn to convert letter combinations into sounds. Check the Glossary, pages 71–2, for a definition if you don't understand the headings.

APPENDIX B — NONSENSE COMBINATIONS AND SOUND GROUPS

HOW TO USE NONSENSE COMBINATIONS

Each group is categorised.

Take one group at a time and write each word in red texta on a flashcard. Flashcards can be made from firm cardboard and should be approximately 10 cm long and 8 cm high. Write the letter combination largely and clearly.

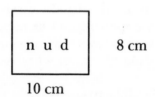

Sit opposite the child with a card facing up in your hand, so that you can see the nonsense word.

Twist the card as you lay it on the table in front of the child so the child can see it.

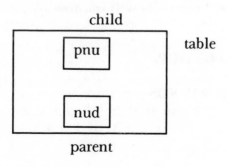

Ask the child to look at the card and say it. If children falter or give an incorrect sound, get them to look at your lips as you say 'nud' slowly and clearly. Don't let them falter or stumble too long. Simply tell them what the sound is and ask them to repeat it. Repeat again if necessary.

If the child makes more than three errors in a particular group, only do that one group that night. When you've worked through a group, pick up the cards, shuffle them, and repeat the teaching procedure. Your teaching technique should be 'stress free' for the child. It should resemble a game. Ten minutes each night will be sufficient.

If you have 5 to 6 sessions a week your child will absorb what is being taught. Don't be concerned if it takes a few weeks for your child to master this activity. It may take 4 to 5 weeks to work through the groups below.

However, **it is absolutely essential that sounds be mastered before spelling can be taught successfully**.

Our experience shows that, after a while, the child will utilise in reading at school what is being learnt in these exercises.

Once your child can correctly sound out all the groups below you can return to page 13 of the main text, confident that you can now introduce the spelling technique to your child. Remember that the spelling technique is not effective with children who cannot master the tasks on page 11. Just be patient and take it one step at a time. Your child will improve.

SOUND GROUPS

SINGLE SOUNDS

m b p h f k d t c g j
y s r w n l x z v

INITIAL VOWEL SOUNDS

a e i o u

Gp 1	Gp 2	Gp 3	Gp 4	Gp 5	Gp 6
ef	ag	am	ad	et	op
af	og	im	id	ot	ip
if	ig	um	od	ut	ap
	eg	om	ud	it	ep
uf	ug	em	ed	at	up

If the child asks, 'Where is *of*?' explain that this is a special word in English that is pronounced *ov*.

SHORT MIDDLE VOWEL SOUNDS

Gp 1	Gp 2	Gp 3	Gp 4	Gp 5	Gp 6
dab	wob	tud	hig	ned	jom
dob	wub	tid	heg	nad	jem
dub	wib	ted	hag	nod	jam
dib	web	tad	hog	nud	jim
deb	wab	tod	hug	nid	jum

LONG MIDDLE VOWEL SOUNDS

Gp 1	Gp 2	Gp 3	Gp 4	Gp 5	Gp 6
date	tite	nute	sute	bote	gete
dete	tote	note	site	bete	gote
dite	tute	nite	sate	bate	gite
dote	tete	nete	sete	bite	gute
dute	tate	nate	sote	bute	gate

SEEING AND SAYING THE DIFFERENCE BETWEEN SHORT AND LONG MIDDLE VOWEL SOUNDS

	a	e	i	o	u
Short	gat	nep	tip	hot	dup
Long	gate	nepe	tipe	hote	dupe
Short	bab	met	mit	tot	mub
Long	babe	mete	mite	tote	mube

| *Short* | hat | reb | rib | fob | nut |
| *Long* | hate | rebe | ribe | fobe | nute |

| *Short* | pat | len | sip | nob | lun |
| *Long* | pate | lene | sipe | nobe | lune |

INITIAL CONSONANT BLENDS AND DIGRAPHS

Gp 1	*Gp 2*	*Gp 3*	*Gp 4*	*Gp 5*	*Gp 6*
clod	spom	smop	drot	slat	prat
gron	tron	flig	shup	spin	stun
shog	crid	slin	snop	swot	flup
chig	shed	steg	brit	whon	grot
slig	slod	craw	stip	glup	slob
spen	pleg	clit	quin	sput	fleb

FINAL CONSONANT BLENDS AND DIGRAPHS

Gp 1	*Gp 2*	*Gp 3*	*Gp 4*	*Gp 5*	*Gp 6*
nang	bath	peck	sunt	luft	bund
tush	selt	menk	bung	dush	mift
dask	feng	wuth	sith	bish	bick
dend	kest	wuch	bisk	sect	fest
memp	hasp	nush	deng	gesh	lenk
narch	lang	tass	feld	lert	geg
hesk	beck	leth	hung	dunk	nuck

VOWEL DIGRAPHS AND DIPHTHONGS
MIXED WITH SOME SHORT AND LONG VOWEL
SOUNDS

Gp 1	*Gp 2*	*Gp 3*	*Gp 4*	*Gp 5*	*Gp 6*
roon	iet	poot	keat	loat	deet
nean	roan	norn	jake	teel	lail
loot	jite	jeet	kole	poil	fane
mort	marm	neek	koon	noan	toin
fike	huck	rook	nend	pow	gowl
worn	fown	poon	geed	neard	nind

APPENDIX C—
PARENTS' CHECKLIST

	ALWAYS	SOMETIMES	FORGOTTEN
1. We work in a very quiet room away from other children and household noises.			
2. I sit opposite the child across a table.			
3. We use blank paper.			
4. We use a bold red or yellow felt pen.			
5. I write words no less than 40 mm (1¾″) in height.			
6. I break the word, working from both ends.			
7. I separate double consonants.			
8. I separate silent letters.			
9. I relax the child before teaching begins.			
10. I offer the child an incentive to come to each session.			
11. I pre-test words before I start each teaching session.			
12. I watch the child's eye and body movements.			

	ALWAYS	SOMETIMES	FORGOTTEN
13. I ignore all the errors the child makes, and don't comment on them.			
14. Each session is made stress free for the child.			
15. I re-focus the child's gaze by tapping one finger loudly next to the part of the word exposed.			
16. When the child stumbles, I don't delay in intervening and telling the child the correct pronunciation.			
17. When I offer the child a correct pronunciation, I say, 'Watch my lips as I say it,' and then I ask the child to imitate.			
18. As I expose the parts of words to be learnt I count 'one hundred, two hundred, three hundred' silently to allow for slow exposure and effective learning.			
19. I ask the child to write the words down in 'the parts in which you have learnt them', instead of in full words.			

	ALWAYS	SOMETIMES	FORGOTTEN
20. I do not ask my student to spell a word aloud.			
21. In the event of a memory block I say to the child, 'Close your eyes and try to see the word part as I tap it.'			
22. I tap out the word, each part separately, on the palm of the hand that the child writes with as I say the word part.			
23. I keep each session to a time limit with which the child can cope, about 15 minutes maximum per day.			
24. At the end of each session I say how much I have enjoyed working with the child.			
25. To finish the session I give my child a hug or cuddle.			

Each of these things should occur in each session. If you've found an item that you've missed, review your technique and be conscious of it in the next session. A small omission could make the difference between success or failure. It's like the small mechanical fault that prevents your car from working!

APPENDIX D— SUMMARY OF TECHNIQUE FOR TEACHING SPELLING

THE THEORY

1. The method is based on an integrative approach: vision, sound, movement, recall, touch and rhythm being used together.
2. The rate of learning is **slowed down** to 3 seconds per unit of information.
3. Visual distractions and difficulties are minimised by the use of:
   - blank paper
   - colour red or yellow pen
   - large lettering
   - gradual exposure of each unit of information
   - the teaching position (opposite the child).
4. Rules of syllabification are not strictly adhered to.
5. Repetition.
6. Errors are ignored. Reinforce correct responses and re-teach incorrect responses.
7. The technique doesn't rely on average short term memory of what was heard in sequence.

THE TECHNIQUE

1. Pre-test to determine unknown words.
2. On a *blank white* page write the word in full and break up the word.
3. Method for breaking up the word is:
   (1) Identify parts easiest to remember.
   (2) Work from both ends.

(3) Separate double consonants.

(4) Space parts of words across the page, e.g.

accommodate

ac	com	mo	date
Pt1	Pt2	Pt3	Pt4

4. Actual teaching routine:

(1) Sit opposite the child.

(2) Cover the broken-up word. Ask the child to say the *full* word. If unable to do so, the parent says it, reads it aloud and has the child repeat it.

(3) Cover the full word with one piece of paper while, with a separate piece of paper, cover Parts 2 to 4.

(4) Have the child look at Part 1, and say it (silently count 'one hundred, two hundred, three hundred'). If the child is unable to pronounce/blend it, tell the child what it is. Child repeats.

(5) Cover Parts 1, 3 and 4. Expose Part 2. Repeat procedure in (4).

(6) Repeat procedure for Parts 3 and 4.

(7) Recommence at Part 1 and work through the word again, part by part, as above.

(8) Place a piece of blank paper over the word, then:
   - give the child a pen, and
   - ask the child to write the word 'accommodate' **in the parts** in which it has been learnt, keeping a space between the parts.

(9) Immediately the child is stuck and has a memory block:
   - ask the child to close eyes,
   - relax the child,
   - take the child's hand and slowly tap out the parts of the word twice in succession,
   - ask the child to rewrite the word twice.

(10) This switching of channel, from the eyes to touch and hearing seems to unblock the memory effectively by slowing down the brain and enabling it to re-cue.

(11) If the error recurs, teach the word again, as in (4)–(7) above.

(12) Next day:
- review the words taught (pre-test),
- re-teach words wrongly spelled,
- introduce new words for the day, and
- teach using steps (1)–(8).

GLOSSARY — TECHNICAL TERMS USED IN SPELLING AND READING

The English language is one of the most complicated languages in the world. The following guide to the terminology used in the teaching of spelling and reading may be helpful to parents who are working with their children.

complex word   A complex word is one that has both a prefix and suffix added to the root, e.g. in the complex word **imperfection, im** is the prefix, **perfect** is the root and **ion** is the suffix.

compound word   These are words made up of two independent words joined together to make a new word. Each word contributing to the compound word keeps its separate form, e.g. steamship which is a compound word made from the two words, steam and ship. Others are blackbird, strawberry, dustbin and mainland.

digraph   These are two letters used together to spell a single sound, e.g. **ea** in **each, th** in wi**th, sh** in **shop, ck** in ba**ck, ee** in k**ee**p, **oo** in m**oo**n.

diphthong   A vowel sound made up of two vowel sounds pronounced in one syllable is called a diphthong, e.g. **ou** in h**ou**se, **oi** in n**oi**se, **ea** in f**ea**r, **ai** in h**ai**r.

final blend   These occur when two consonants at the end of a word join together to make a sound, e.g. re**st**, stu**mp**, mi**nt**, ha**nd**, gi**ft**, de**sk**, be**lt**, ba**nk**, mi**lk**, fa**ct**, he**lp**, ke**pt**, ra**ng**, si**ng**.

homophone   This is a word having the same pronunciation as another word but with a different meaning and origin, e.g. **ate** and **eight** are homophones. Some others are **road, rode** and **rowed; saw, sore** and **soar.**

initial blend   These occur when a word starts with two consonants that make a sound, e.g. **sl**it, **sm**og, **st**op, **sp**ot, **sc**at, **sk**in, **sw**am, **sn**ag, **bl**uff, **cl**ass, **fl**ag, **gl**ass, **pl**an, **br**ing, **cr**op, **dr**op, **pr**am, **tr**am, **wh**ip, **fr**og, **tw**in.

long vowel sound   These are heard when the sound of the vowel changes to a softer sound as in m**a**te, P**e**te, w**i**ne, n**o**te, c**u**te. Note that this softer vowel sound usually occurs when there is a vowel at the end of the word.

prefix   A prefix is a syllable or word put at the *beginning* of a word to change its meaning or to make another word, e.g. **pre** as in **pre**paid. Some other examples are **re**place, **re**open, **in**door, **pre**view, **sub**ject, **con**ceal, **ad**dress, **dis**comfort and **anti**dote.

short vowel sound   These are sharp sounds made by the letters, **a, e, i, o, u,** similar to the sounds in the following words: m**a**t, p**e**t, w**i**n, n**o**t, c**u**t.

silent letter   Silent letters are letters that are included in a word but do not make a sound, e.g. com**b**, sc**i**ence, **g**nome, **h**onest, kni**t**ting, sal**m**on, autum**n**, nes**t**le and **w**rong. Some words in English end in a silent letter, for example smok**e**.

single sound   This is the sound that a single letter of the alphabet makes, e.g. the letter **c** makes a 'c' sound as in **c**at.

suffix   A suffix is a syllable or word put at the *end* of a word to change its meaning or to make another word, such as adding **ly** to bad to make bad**ly**, **ness** to good to make good**ness** and **ful** to spoon so it becomes spoon**ful**. Some others are **ment** as in amaze**ment**, **able** as in enjoy**able**, **en** as in froz**en**, **ence** as in abs**ence** and **ant** to make import**ant**.

triple blend   These are formed when three consonants at the beginning of a word make a sound, e.g. **scr**ap, **spl**ash, **str**ip, **thr**ow, **spr**ing.